# I Am Wind

To all who have fought and failed
against the Wind
— RP

To my husband, Jeffrey —
the wind that guides me.
— RW

Text copyright © 2024 by Rachel Poliquin
Illustrations copyright © 2024 by Rachel Wada

Tundra Books, an imprint of Tundra Book Group, a division of Penguin Random House of Canada Limited

Library and Archives Canada Cataloguing in Publication

Title: I am wind / written by Rachel Poliquin ; illustrated by Rachel Wada.
Names: Poliquin, Rachel, 1975- author. | Wada, Rachel, illustrator.
Identifiers: Canadiana (print) 2022048547X | Canadiana (ebook) 20220485488 | ISBN 9780735272187 (hardcover) | ISBN 9780735272194 (EPUB)
Subjects: LCSH: Winds — Juvenile literature. | LCSH: Winds — Folklore. | LCGFT: Instructional and educational works.
Classification: LCC QC931.4 .P65 2024 | DDC j551.51/8 — dc23

Published simultaneously in the United States of America by Tundra Books of Northern New York, an imprint of Tundra Book Group, a division of Penguin Random House of Canada Limited

Library of Congress Control Number: 2022950959

Edited by Elizabeth Kribs
Designed by Sophie Paas-Lang
The artwork in this book was created with both traditional and digital mediums of brush and ink and photoshop.
The text was set in Garamond Premier Pro and Metallophile.

Printed in India

www.penguinrandomhouse.ca

1 2 3 4 5    28 27 26 25 24

Penguin
Random House
TUNDRA BOOKS
tundra

# I Am Wind

Written by
## Rachel Poliquin

Illustrated by
## Rachel Wada

tundra

# CONTENTS

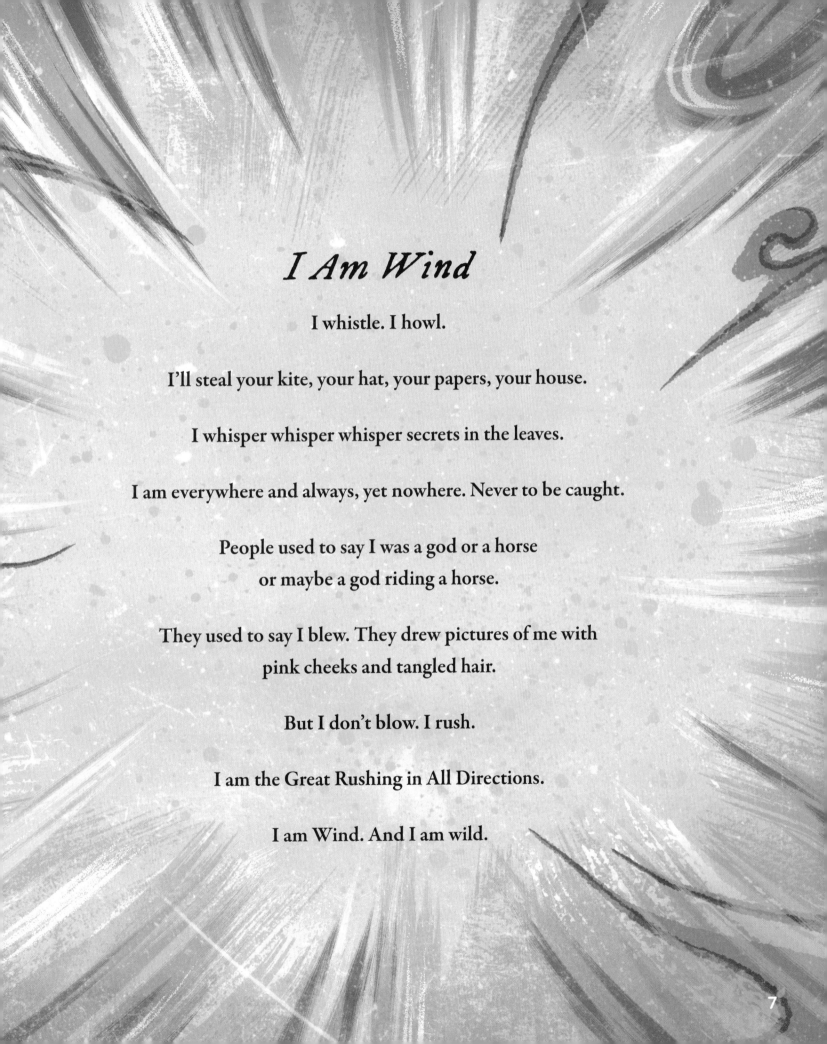

# I Am Wind

I whistle. I howl.

I'll steal your kite, your hat, your papers, your house.

I whisper whisper whisper secrets in the leaves.

I am everywhere and always, yet nowhere. Never to be caught.

People used to say I was a god or a horse
or maybe a god riding a horse.

They used to say I blew. They drew pictures of me with
pink cheeks and tangled hair.

But I don't blow. I rush.

I am the Great Rushing in All Directions.

I am Wind. And I am wild.

**WIND GODS AND DEMONS** are found across different cultures.

The Chinese wind goddess **FENG PO PO** rides a tiger through the clouds with her winds stuffed in a bag.

The Iroquois god of the west wind is **DAJOJI**, a fierce panther.

**PAKA'A** carries the winds of the Hawaiian Islands in a gourd along with his grandmother's bones.

The fang-beaked **EHECATL**, the Aztec god of air and wind, once destroyed the entire world.

With winged feet and an icy beard, the Greek god **BOREAS** blows cold wind from the north.

The Hindu god of winds, **VAYU**, rides a golden gazelle.

The four-winged Sumerian wind demon, **PAZUZU**, brings famine from the southwest during droughts.

# EVERYWHERE AND ALWAYS

You can usually find me in uneven places, where mountains rise and oceans begin, and always, always where hot meets cold.

If our planet were all flat and the sun shone evenly and the airs rose smoothly, I would be dull. But our planet isn't flat, and the sun doesn't shine evenly. There are hot places and cold places, oceans and deserts, tall mountains and tight valleys that bottle me like a tiger in a jar until I explode in fury.

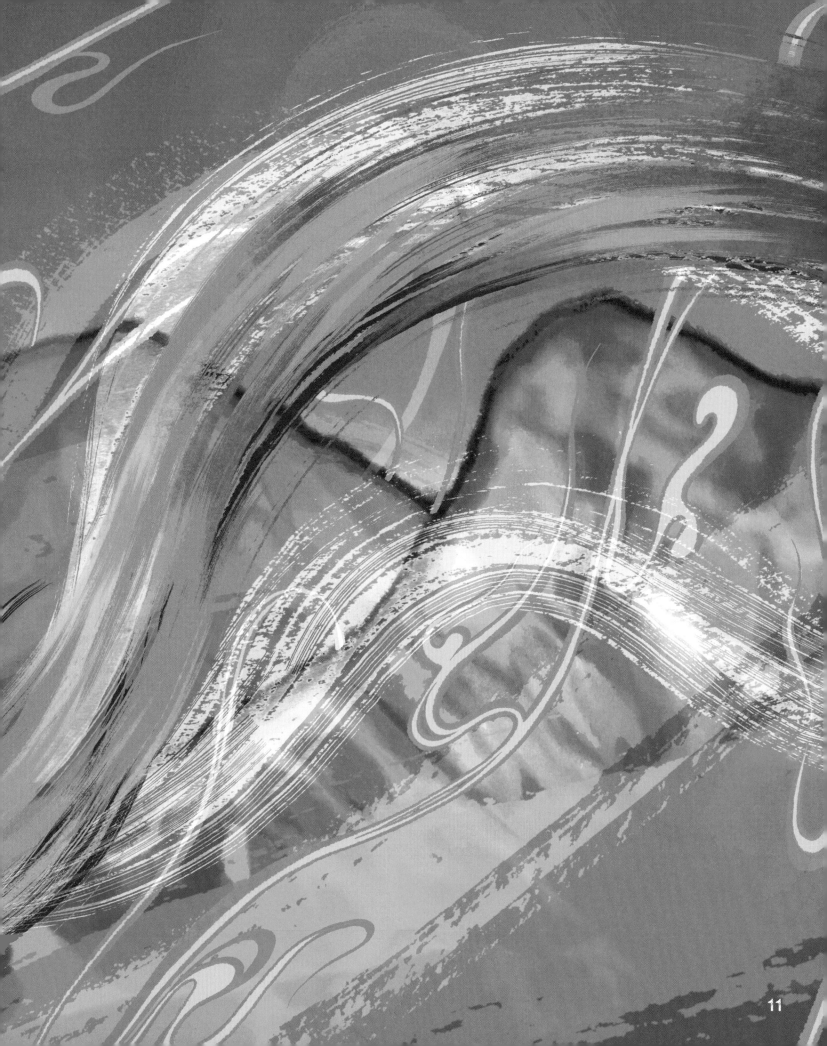

As air warms, it becomes lighter and rises upward.
Cooler air is sucked into the space where the warm air
used to be. This movement of air is WIND.

HIGH PRESSURE

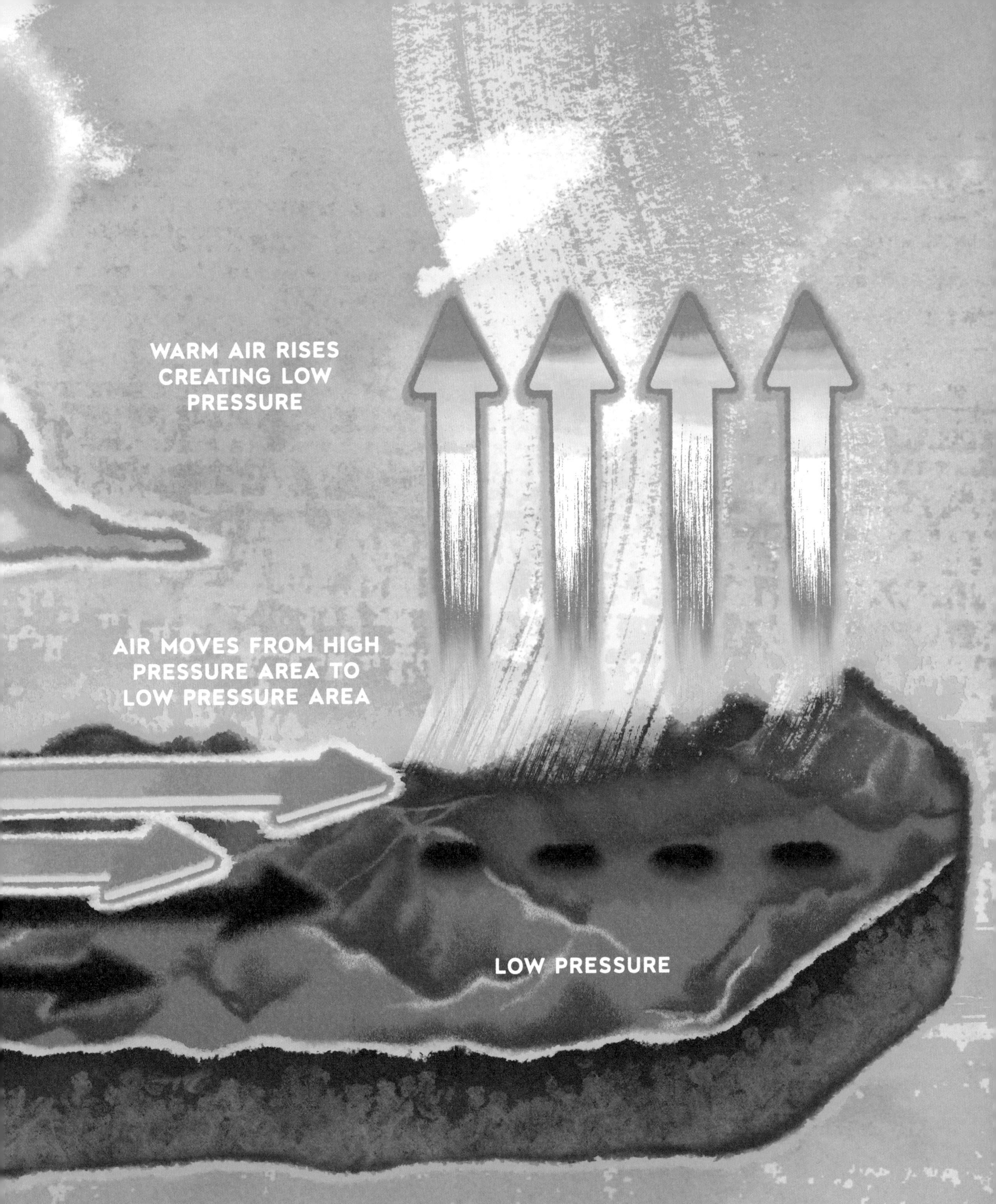

WARM AIR RISES
CREATING LOW
PRESSURE

AIR MOVES FROM HIGH
PRESSURE AREA TO
LOW PRESSURE AREA

LOW PRESSURE

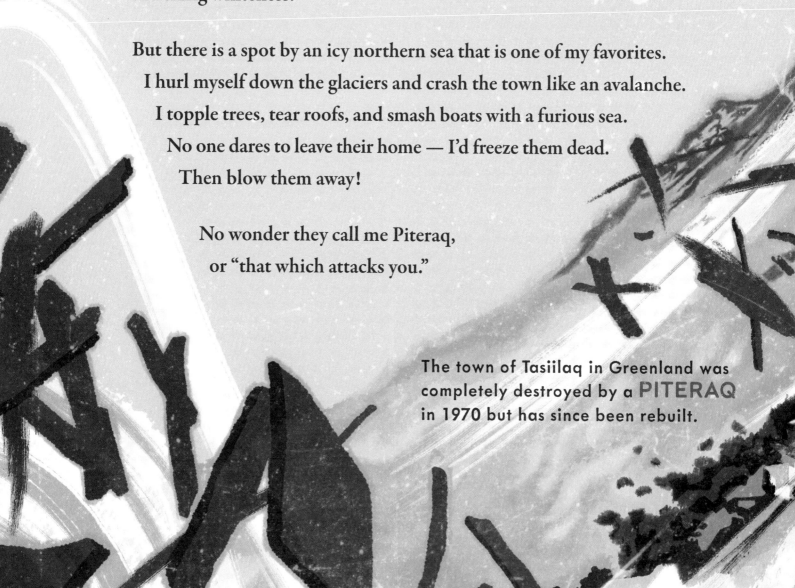

# ICE DRAGONS

I love tall, snowy mountain peaks. I thunder down their slopes, hard and fast and furious, breathing ice like a frozen dragon. I get wilder, colder, faster, faster as I squeeze myself through the mountain valleys.

I'm famously wild on the frozen slopes around the South Pole. I am always rushing down those glaciers, always whipping up snow into blinding, shrieking whiteness.

But there is a spot by an icy northern sea that is one of my favorites.
I hurl myself down the glaciers and crash the town like an avalanche.
I topple trees, tear roofs, and smash boats with a furious sea.
No one dares to leave their home — I'd freeze them dead.
Then blow them away!

No wonder they call me Piteraq,
or "that which attacks you."

The town of Tasiilaq in Greenland was completely destroyed by a PITERAQ in 1970 but has since been rebuilt.

14

**KATABATIC WINDS**, such as the Piteraq, use gravity to drag cold air down from icy mountain slopes. They usually occur near coastlines and can reach incredible speeds of up to 186 miles per hour (300 kilometers per hour). Antarctica is the windiest continent, and blizzards are common at any time of year. Other famous katabatic winds are the Bora in Europe and the Oroshi in Japan.

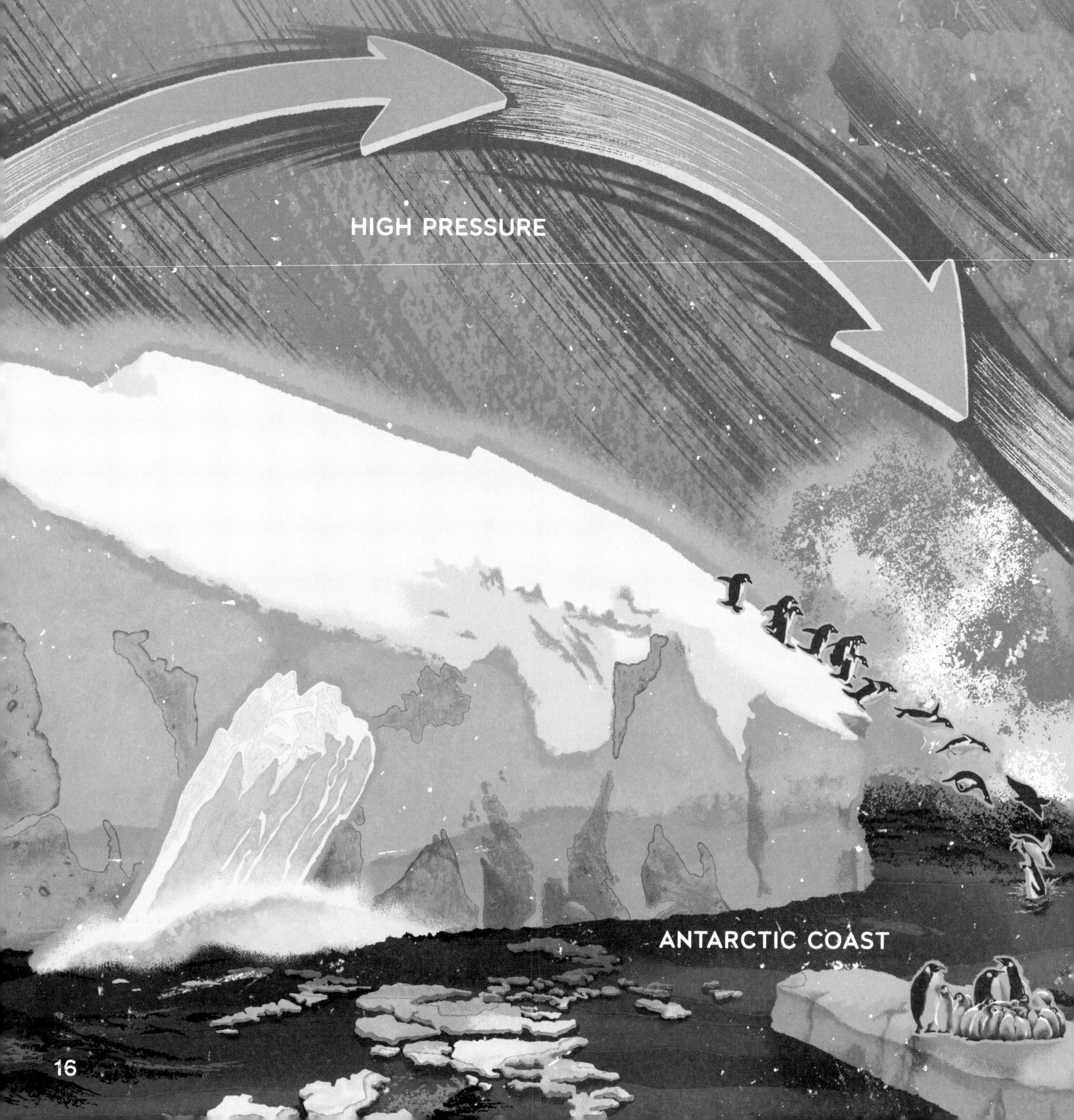

HIGH PRESSURE

ANTARCTIC COAST

DIFFERENCE IN
PRESSURE FORCES AIR
TO MOVE QUICKLY

LOW PRESSURE

SOUTHERN OCEAN

# SNOW EATER

My mountain winds aren't always ice dragons. Sometimes I'll bring a treat down the mountain — spring in the middle of winter. Just for a day.

When warm airs butt into tall mountains, they push their way up the sides. The higher they climb, the colder and drier they become. Then sometimes, at the very top — if the airs are perfectly crisp and dry, and the mountain slope is perfectly steep and narrow — I feel that giddy spark, and I rush, rush, rush down the other side, getting hotter and faster as I go.

When I rush hot down the Rocky Mountains into the Great Plains below, they call me Chinook. I come in winter like a summer wind, melting icicles, turning snowmen to puddles. People say I bring joy and headaches too, but I don't know about that.

Then, snap! I'm gone. And the bitter chill returns.

FOEHN WINDS, like the Chinook, are dry, downslope winds on the leeward, or rain shadow, side of mountains. They can blow at speeds of 150 miles per hour (240 kilometers per hour). The name was originally coined for the Foehn winds in the Alps. On the eastern slopes of the Andes in Argentina, they are called the Zonda.

The Māori of New Zealand tell a story of how the winds and storm clouds were created.

In the earliest times, Mother Earth (known as Papatūānuku) and Father Sky (Ranginui) held each other tightly. Without any space between earth and sky, there was no light, only darkness. Papa and Rangi had many sons, who were forced to live in the cramped darkness between them until, at last, the sons decided to tear their parents apart. The brothers all agreed except for Tāwhirimātea, the father of winds and storms.

Each son tried to split his parents, and each failed. Finally, Tāne Mahuta, the god of forests and birds, planted his feet firmly on Papa and pushed up on Rangi as hard as he could. His parents cried out, but he kept pushing Mother Earth down beneath

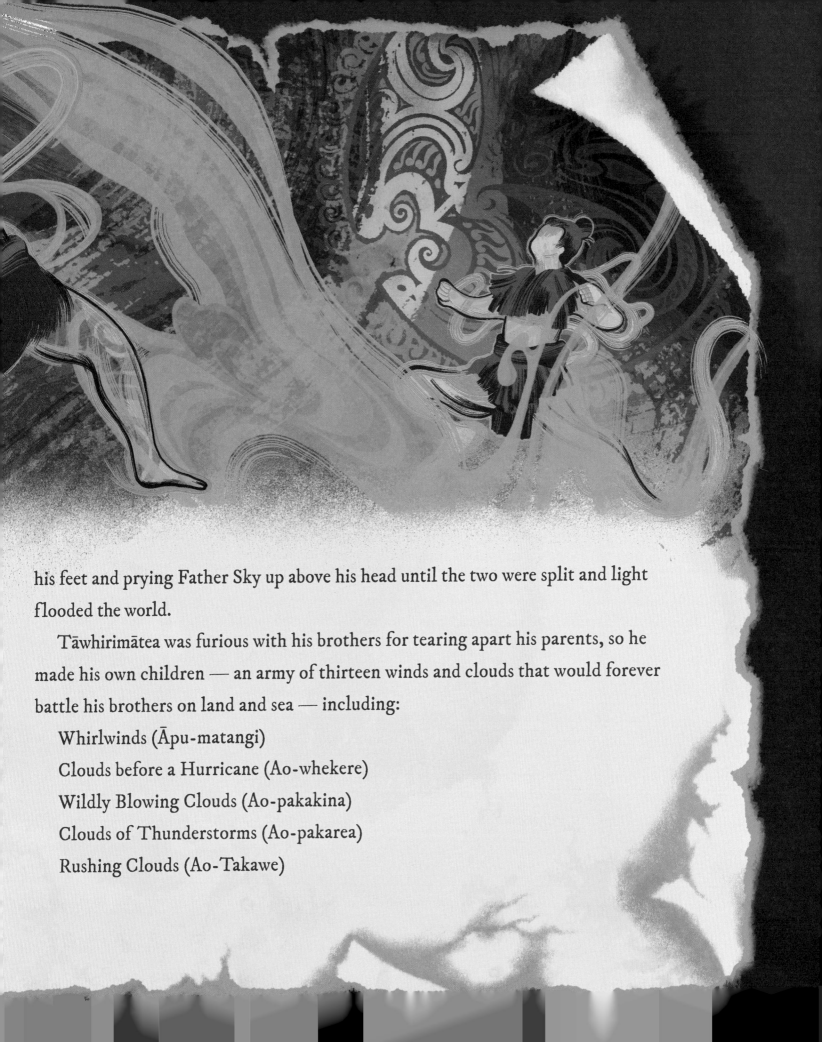

his feet and prying Father Sky up above his head until the two were split and light
flooded the world.

Tāwhirimātea was furious with his brothers for tearing apart his parents, so he
made his own children — an army of thirteen winds and clouds that would forever
battle his brothers on land and sea — including:

Whirlwinds (Āpu-matangi)

Clouds before a Hurricane (Ao-whekere)

Wildly Blowing Clouds (Ao-pakakina)

Clouds of Thunderstorms (Ao-pakarea)

Rushing Clouds (Ao-Takawe)

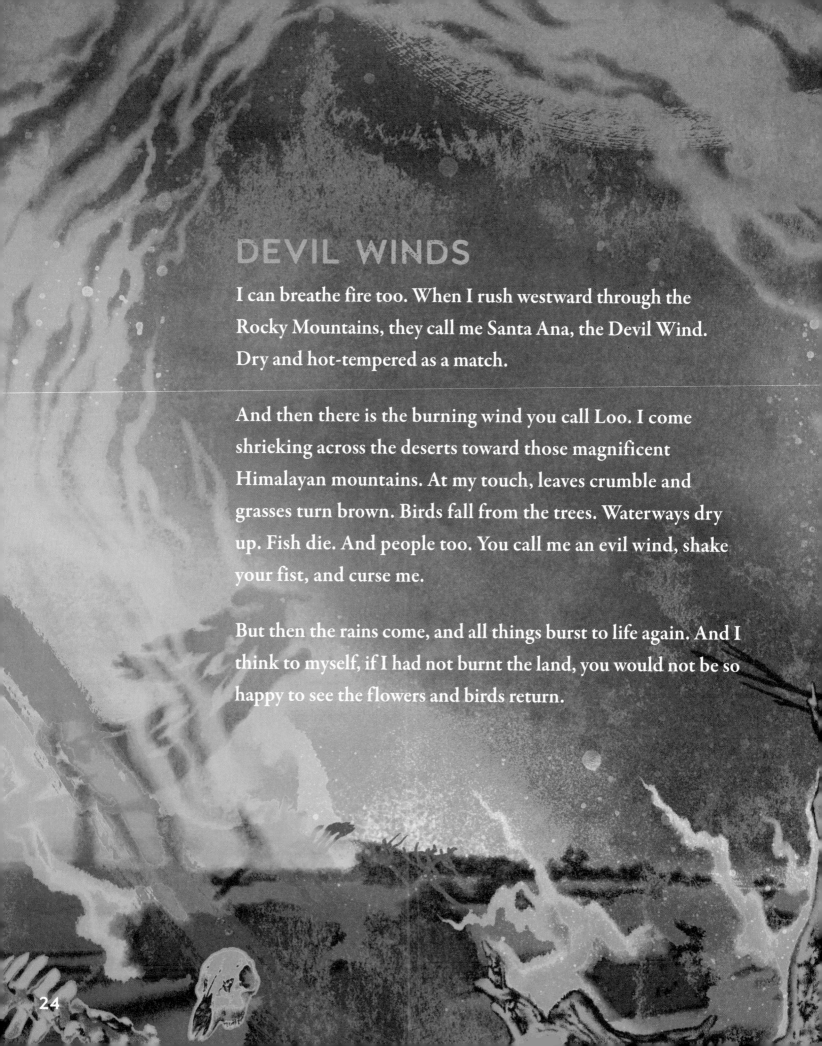

## DEVIL WINDS

I can breathe fire too. When I rush westward through the Rocky Mountains, they call me Santa Ana, the Devil Wind. Dry and hot-tempered as a match.

And then there is the burning wind you call Loo. I come shrieking across the deserts toward those magnificent Himalayan mountains. At my touch, leaves crumble and grasses turn brown. Birds fall from the trees. Waterways dry up. Fish die. And people too. You call me an evil wind, shake your fist, and curse me.

But then the rains come, and all things burst to life again. And I think to myself, if I had not burnt the land, you would not be so happy to see the flowers and birds return.

The searing hot and dry LOO is said to make an eerie shrieking sound as it blows north-eastward across Pakistan and northern India toward the Himalayas in early summer. Temperatures can reach 120 degrees Fahrenheit (50 degrees Celsius) and can cause fatal heatstroke.

25

The SANTA ANA winds begin when cold, dry air from the high deserts in Nevada and Utah in the southwestern United States is forced down through the mountain valleys toward the coast of California. As the desert air rushes through the tight canyons, it accelerates, heats up (at about 30 degrees Fahrenheit per mile/10 degrees Celsius per kilometer), and becomes even drier. The winds usually come at the end of summer, during the fire season.

SOUTHERN
CALIFORNIA COAST

THE WIND
BECOMES
HOTTER, FASTER
AND DRIER AS
IT CONTINUES
DOWNSLOPE

COLD, DRY AIR IN THE HIGH INLAND DESERTS

THE COLD, HEAVY AIR SINKS DOWN THROUGH CANYONS

AS THE AIR DESCENDS, IT IS COMPRESSED AND WARMS RAPIDLY

# WARM EMBRACE

I am not always so fierce. Do you know Zephyrus, my west wind?

The people of the Greek Islands told stories of four brothe who blew from the four points of the compass. Boreas from the North with a beard full of icicles. Notus rushing stormy from the South. Eurus from the East bringing autumn with him. And gentle Zephryus from the West, bringing soft breezes and warm rains, scattering flowers in springtime. The Greeks drew pictures of him as a beautiful man with wings. Some said he was married to the goddess of rainbows Some said he was the father of fruits.

I am not a god with wings. But I do sing through the forests and bend grasses to waves of gold. I gather seeds and carry them far away and set birds spinning, diving, soaring, rising.

**PREVAILING WINDS** are winds that blow from a single direction over a particular part of the world. They often have a distinct character since they can carry features (such as temperature, moisture, dust, seeds) from the lands they pass over.

Many trees and plants have **SEEDS** that are made to be caught and spread by the wind. Some seeds look like parachutes or helicopters. Some glide or flutter. Others tumble along the ground or fill the air with cottony seeds like snow.

The **TOWER OF THE WINDS** was built in Athens two thousand years ago to honor the Greek gods of wind. The octagonal tower is 40 feet (12 meters) tall and once had a water clock, a sundial, and a wind vane. A wind god was carved on each of the eight sides.

# ODYSSEUS AND THE BAG OF WINDS

There once was a long and terrible war between the people of Greece and the city of Troy. One of the Greek warriors was named Odysseus. It was Odysseus who thought up the trick of hiding soldiers inside a giant wooden horse, which finally defeated the Trojans. But before the Greeks left, they destroyed Troy, ruined its temples, and treated its people so badly that they angered the gods.

Unaware of what was to come, Odysseus and his men set sail for home. On their way, they stopped at the island of Aeolia, where Odysseus's friend Aeolus was king and Keeper of the Winds. As a gift, Aeolus gathered all the wild and dangerous winds into an ox-hide sack and gave it to Odysseus, leaving free only the steady west wind to speed his friend's journey home.

Odysseus hid the sack carefully on his boat. For nine days, the fleet traveled smoothly with the west wind in their sails, and soon their homeland was in sight.

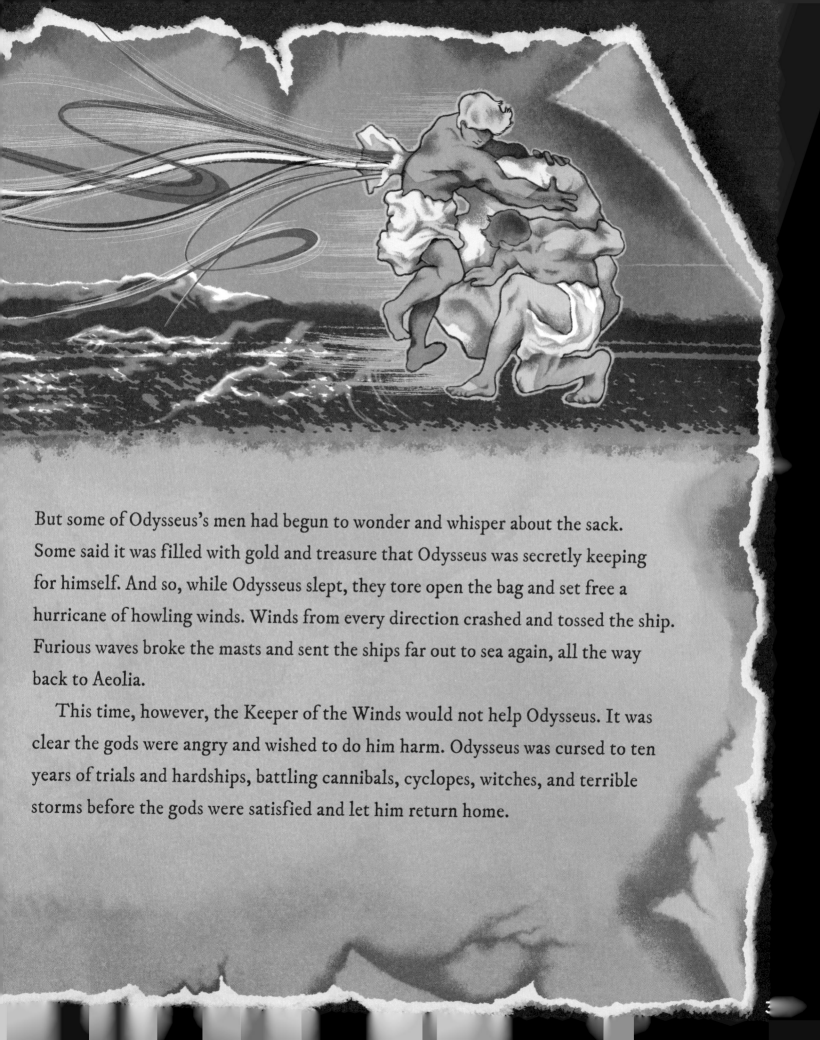

But some of Odysseus's men had begun to wonder and whisper about the sack. Some said it was filled with gold and treasure that Odysseus was secretly keeping for himself. And so, while Odysseus slept, they tore open the bag and set free a hurricane of howling winds. Winds from every direction crashed and tossed the ship. Furious waves broke the masts and sent the ships far out to sea again, all the way back to Aeolia.

This time, however, the Keeper of the Winds would not help Odysseus. It was clear the gods were angry and wished to do him harm. Odysseus was cursed to ten years of trials and hardships, battling cannibals, cyclopes, witches, and terrible storms before the gods were satisfied and let him return home.

# OCEAN BREEZES

I like when you celebrate me with kites. Giant lobsters, wheeling polka dots, sea serpents — you know I'll come, especially by the seashore. I'll blow in from the sea during the day and out again at dusk, dancing the kites into kaleidoscope skies. Whistling and spinning, pulling higher, higher, higher still, then . . . snap! They're mine.

I can be gentle, but always remember that my heart is wild.

**OCEAN BREEZES** often occur at shorelines. Because land heats up faster than the ocean, warm air rises over the land during the daytime, which pulls cooler air from across the water into shore. When the sun sets and the temperature drops, the ocean retains its warmth better than land, so the breeze reverses, blowing from the cooler land out across a warmer ocean.

Dozens of KITE FESTIVALS are held around the world. The beachside festival in Cervia, Italy, is known for its fanciful and artistic kites.

Some kite festivals are competitive,
like the Hamamatsu Festival in Japan,
where the kites do battle in the air.

The Barriletes Gigantes festival in Guatemala raises massive circular kites on All Saints' Day to carry messages to the loved ones who have passed or ward off bad spirits.

# INVISIBLE YET ALL-POWERFUL

What is gentle? What is fierce? I am everywhere and always. All-powerful, yet never to be seen. And I bring things to life.

My breath bewitches your hair, your hat, your papers skittering forever beyond your grasp. I give moaning voices to empty spaces. I whip the waves into an army. I sway your chimes with ghostly longing.

And then I am gone. And all falls silent and lifeless once more.

In 1805, Francis Beaufort created a wind scale that ships could use to describe weather conditions at sea. At the time, all ships were powered by wind, yet there were no instruments to measure its speed. Since wind is invisible, Beaufort looked carefully at its effects on the sea. Later, THE BEAUFORT SCALE was expanded to estimate wind speeds on land.

**0 · CALM**
sea like a mirror

**1 · LIGHT AIR**
ripples like scales on the surface

**2 · LIGHT BREEZE**
small wavelets with glassy crests

**3 · GENTLE BREEZE**
large wavelets; crests begin to break

**4 · MODERATE BREEZE**
small waves with some white crests

**5 · FRESH BREEZE**
moderate waves with crests; chance of spray

**6 · STRONG BREEZE**
large waves with extensive crests; spray

**7 · NEAR GALE**
sea heaps up with blowing streaks of white foam

**8 · GALE**
waves enlarge; foam blows in dense streaks

## 9 · STRONG GALE
high waves; sea begins to roll

## 10 · STORM
very high waves with overhanging crests; heavy rolling; spray limits visibility

## 11 · VIOLENT STORM
waves so high that ships are hidden between them; foam patches cover the sea

## 12 · HURRICANE
waves over 45 feet (14 meters); sea completely white; air filled with foam

# WIND CHRONICLES
## THE GREAT STORM OF 1703

At the end of 1703, the south of England was hit by a storm so terrible it has been called the Great Storm ever since. (Or at least until the Great Storm of 1987.) The winds came from the west, from across the Atlantic Ocean, and flattened forests of ancient oaks like wheat in the field. Every church steeple in London was torn off. Chimneys collapsed and killed people in their beds. Four hundred windmills were lost; some had spun so wildly, their blades had caught fire. The winds blew seawater at least 15 miles (24 kilometers) inland and coated the trees in thick white salt. The rivers and coastlines flooded, and farm animals were drowned in the fields. One man reported a cow had been blown into a tree.

But the worst was at sea. The weather had been stormy for weeks, so hundreds of ships were crowded together in the English Channel, unable to sail out against the

winds. On the night of the Great Storm, they all crashed together and foundered. It is thought between eight thousand and fifteen thousand lives were lost.

What caused the winds to blow was a great mystery in 1703. Barometers to measure air pressure had recently been invented, and several people noted the air pressure had dropped dramatically — always a sign a storm is on its way. But despite any scientific explanations, great winds were thought to be divine acts by the Christian God. Many people, including the Queen of England, believed the Great Storm had been caused by God's anger with human wickedness. The government ordered a day of fasting for the entire country in the hopes of reminding people to follow the holy path and avoid sins and mischief.

# WIND POWER

Over the centuries, you have found ways to use my power. You build windmills to grind grain or pump water. You covered hillsides with vast forests of turbines for me to play with. With those turbines, I'll power a city. One day, I could power the world . . . if I wanted to.

**WIND POWER** has been used for thousands of years to pump water, chop wood, and grind grain. Wind power is becoming an increasingly important source of renewable energy. The only problem is its inconsistency — if the wind isn't blowing, no electricity is being made.

The **FIRST WINDMILL** to produce electric power was built in 1887 by James Blyth in Scotland. It was 32 feet (10 meters) tall and powered the lights in Blyth's cottage.

The **HORNSEA WIND FARM** on the coast of England is the largest wind farm at sea. It has 174 turbines and covers 157 square miles (407 square kilometers) of the famously wild and windy North Sea. Each turbine is as tall as a thirty-story building and has three 246-foot (75-meter) long blades. Just one rotation of a turbine's blades can power a household for a day, and altogether the farm is expected to power one million homes.

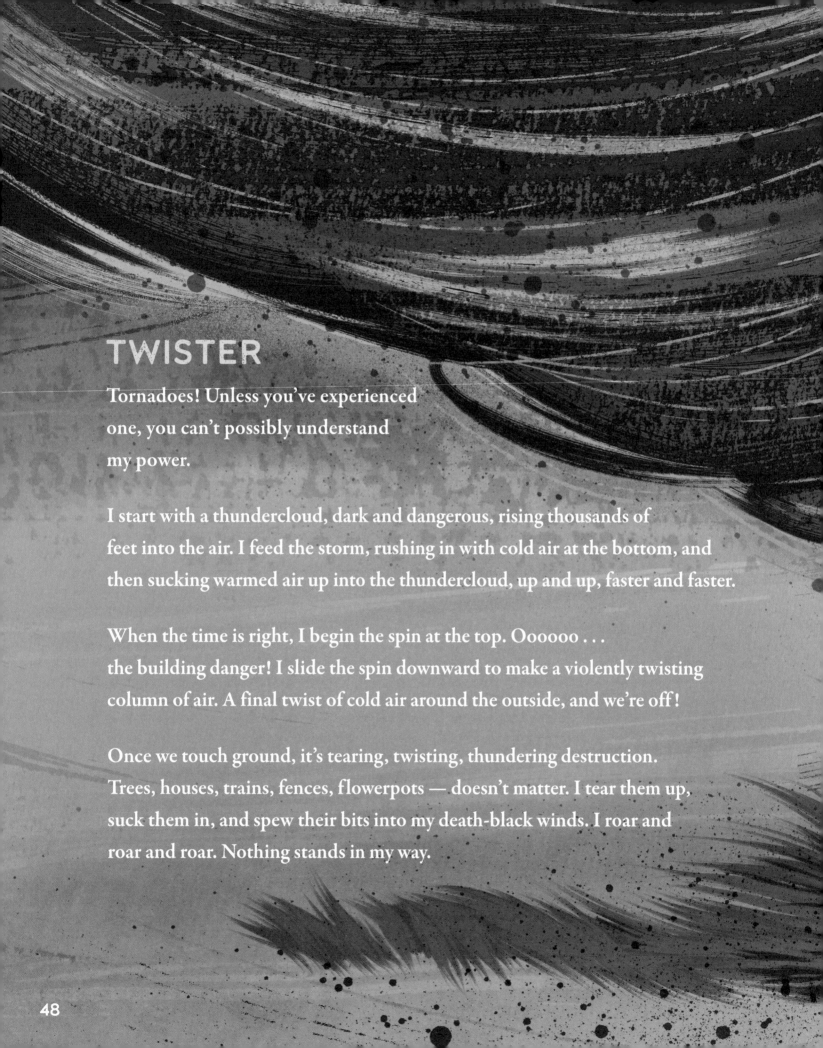

# TWISTER

Tornadoes! Unless you've experienced
one, you can't possibly understand
my power.

I start with a thundercloud, dark and dangerous, rising thousands of
feet into the air. I feed the storm, rushing in with cold air at the bottom, and
then sucking warmed air up into the thundercloud, up and up, faster and faster.

When the time is right, I begin the spin at the top. Oooooo . . .
the building danger! I slide the spin downward to make a violently twisting
column of air. A final twist of cold air around the outside, and we're off!

Once we touch ground, it's tearing, twisting, thundering destruction.
Trees, houses, trains, fences, flowerpots — doesn't matter. I tear them up,
suck them in, and spew their bits into my death-black winds. I roar and
roar and roar. Nothing stands in my way.

**TORNADOES** are violently rotating funnels of air that form inside storms and connect to the ground. They are usually less than a quarter of a mile (half a kilometer) wide and can tear across the ground at tremendous speeds. When they appear over water, they are called waterspouts.

I can't keep it going for long — maybe a minute, maybe an hour. Then I'm spent. The truth is, the twisting makes me strange. I've sucked up chicken houses and set them down without breaking an egg. I've left a toilet on the neighbor's roof.

I'm too wild for your windchasers. They can only measure me afterward, by how much I've destroyed.

Tornadoes can be so violent that their wind speeds are impossible to measure at the time. THE ENHANCED FUJITA SCALE (EFS) rates the intensity of tornadoes based on the amount of damage left behind. The EFS replaced the original Fujita Scale, introduced by Ted Fujita in 1971.

0 · 55-80 MPH
(90-130 KM/H)
large branches broken;
fences blown down;
shingles torn off

1 · 85-110 MPH
(135-175 KM/H)
roofs torn off; flag poles
bent; windows broken

2 · 112-135 MPH
(180-220 KM/H)
telephone poles snap;
walls collapse; trees
uprooted

**3 · 140–165 MPH
(225–265 KM/H)**
walls of schools and
hospitals collapse;
forests flattened

**4 · 168–195 MPH
(270–310 KM/H)**
entire houses blown away

**5 · OVER 195 MPH
(315 KM/H)**
complete destruction

## WIND CHRONICLES
## THE DEADLIEST TORNADO

In the early evening of April 26, 1989, the world's deadliest tornado touched down near the town of Daulatpur in Bangladesh.

It only lasted about an hour, but the mile-wide tornado — known as the Daulatpur-Saturia Tornado — traveled for 50 miles (80 kilometers) and tore through twenty towns and villages, completely destroying everything in its path. Trees were torn up. Homes and buildings were blown apart. The town of Saturia was the worst hit. Nothing was left standing as far as the eye could see. According to reports, the tornado killed at least thirteen hundred people, injured twelve thousand, and left eighty thousand without homes.

Tornadoes in Bangladesh are most common in springtime, just before the monsoon rains begin and the temperatures are the highest. Warm, wet air from the Bay of Bengal flows northward under the cold, dry air coming down from the Himalayas. This causes a very unstable air system (since warm air likes to be above cold air) known as an inversion. Then, when hot, dry air blowing eastward from India pushes into this unstable air, it creates the perfect tornado conditions.

# EARTH SWIRLS

I am wild. But even I must follow rules sometimes.

You know our planet is hot at the middle and cold at the top and bottom. That means warm air is always rising at the middle, and I'm always rushing in with cold air, down from the top and up from the bottom.

But it's not just me that's always rushing. Our planet rushes too. Always spinning around and around itself. As it spins, it drags me along, so as I rush toward the hot middle, I'm pulled with a curve. This means I can usually be found rushing east to west around our planet's middle. You call these my Easterlies. Closer to the poles, I also have my Westerlies, which blow in the opposite direction.

EARTH'S ROTATION

Not so long ago, you needed me at sea. You built boats with towering sails, and I set you on your course. But there is a fine art to harnessing my power. You had better study me carefully. I have sent thousands of ships across oceans. I have sent thousands to the bottom.

NORTH POLE

The influence of Earth's rotation on weather patterns and ocean currents is known as the **CORIOLIS EFFECT.**

EQUATOR

The air is warmer at the equator. This means warm air is always rising at the equator and cooler air is being pulled toward the middle.

Earth is always spinning. Because the planet is wider in the middle than at its top and bottom, the equator is actually spinning faster than the poles.

SOUTH POLE

# SAILING WINDS

**THE TRADE WINDS** are powerful prevailing winds that blow in predictable directions across the seas. Learning their ways was central to early exploration, communication, and trade. Even today, ships follow the trade winds for quick, reliable routes across the oceans.

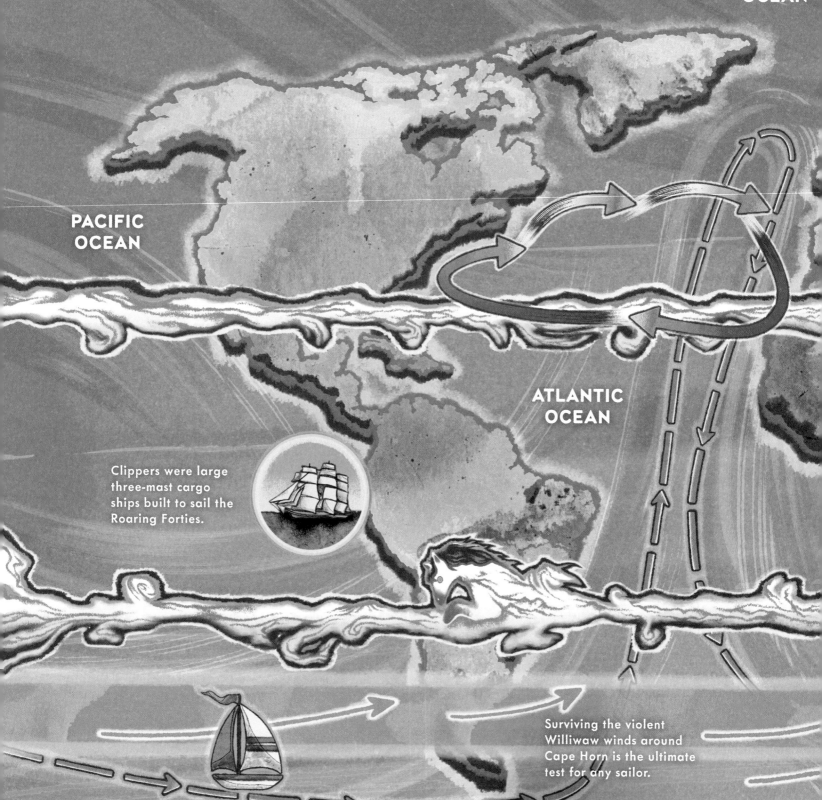

**ARCTIC OCEAN**

**PACIFIC OCEAN**

**ATLANTIC OCEAN**

Clippers were large three-mast cargo ships built to sail the Roaring Forties.

Surviving the violent Williwaw winds around Cape Horn is the ultimate test for any sailor.

Horse latitudes are found around 30 degrees north and south of the equator. Also known as the doldrums, they are famous for calm winds.

The Vendée Globe is the only sailing race that sees participants go around the world, solo, nonstop, and without assistance. Fewer than one hundred people have ever completed the race.

The Roaring Forties are powerful westerly winds. There is little land between 40- and 50-degree latitude to break the winds, so they roar around the world, building power.

Early voyagers used the Trade Winds in their transatlantic crossings. The Easterlies carried the ships toward the Caribbean and the Westerlies brought them back to Europe again.

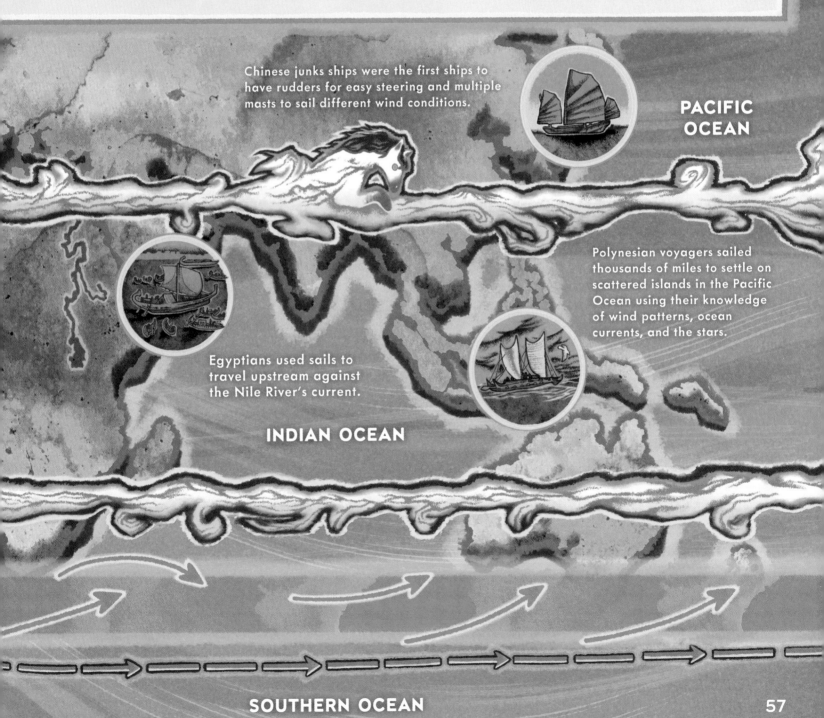

Chinese junks ships were the first ships to have rudders for easy steering and multiple masts to sail different wind conditions.

**PACIFIC OCEAN**

Egyptians used sails to travel upstream against the Nile River's current.

Polynesian voyagers sailed thousands of miles to settle on scattered islands in the Pacific Ocean using their knowledge of wind patterns, ocean currents, and the stars.

**INDIAN OCEAN**

**SOUTHERN OCEAN**

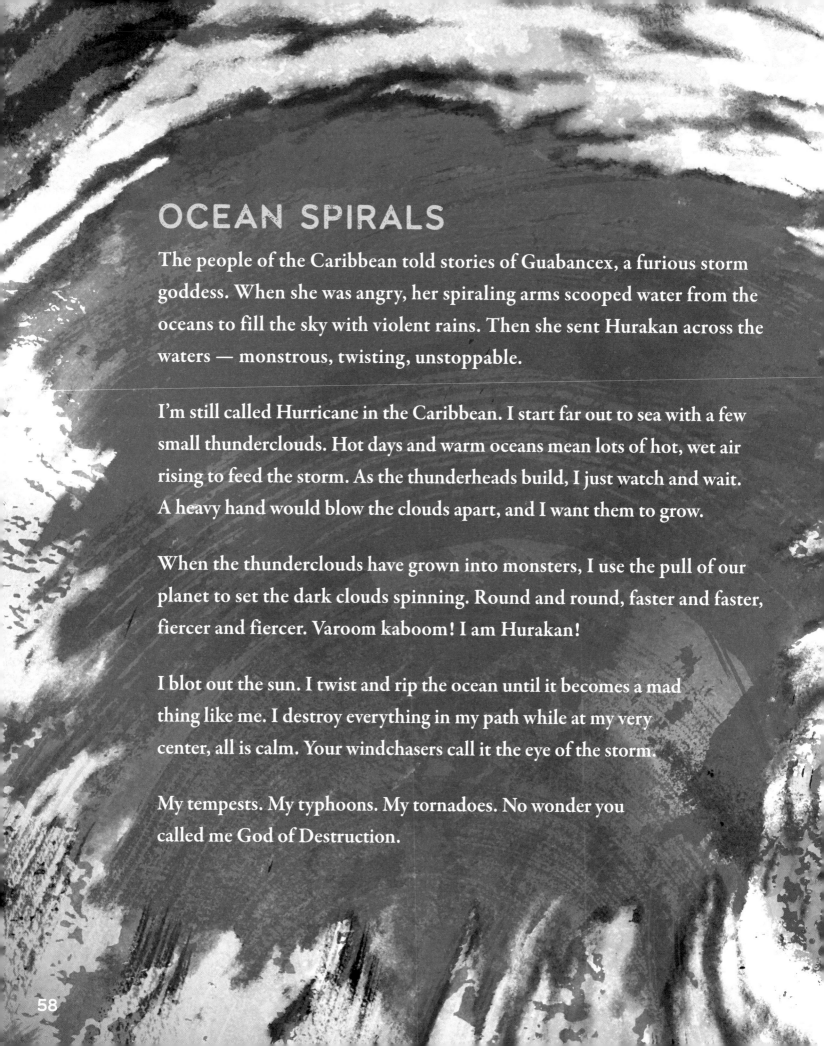

# OCEAN SPIRALS

The people of the Caribbean told stories of Guabancex, a furious storm goddess. When she was angry, her spiraling arms scooped water from the oceans to fill the sky with violent rains. Then she sent Hurakan across the waters — monstrous, twisting, unstoppable.

I'm still called Hurricane in the Caribbean. I start far out to sea with a few small thunderclouds. Hot days and warm oceans mean lots of hot, wet air rising to feed the storm. As the thunderheads build, I just watch and wait. A heavy hand would blow the clouds apart, and I want them to grow.

When the thunderclouds have grown into monsters, I use the pull of our planet to set the dark clouds spinning. Round and round, faster and faster, fiercer and fiercer. Varoom kaboom! I am Hurakan!

I blot out the sun. I twist and rip the ocean until it becomes a mad thing like me. I destroy everything in my path while at my very center, all is calm. Your windchasers call it the eye of the storm.

My tempests. My typhoons. My tornadoes. No wonder you called me God of Destruction.

**CYCLONES** are huge storms fed by warm waters around Earth's equator. They can be **100** to **1,000** miles (160 to 1,600 kilometers) wide and can last for a week or more at sea, but lose power once they touch land. Because of the Coriolis Effect, cyclones spin clockwise in the northern hemisphere and counterclockwise in the southern hemisphere. In the Atlantic, they are called hurricanes. In the Pacific, they are called typhoons.

**STORM SURGES** are massive waves caused by the strong winds circling around the eye of the storm. The rotating winds cause the sea to spin in a vertical column. Once the hurricane hits a coastline's shallow water, the swirling column has nowhere to go but up and inland.

# WIND CHRONICLES
# THE KAMIKAZE WINDS

At the end of the thirteenth century, Kublai Khan, ruler of the Mongol Empire, marched his soldiers across the vast grassy plains of Mongolia toward the sea. First, they conquered Korea. Next, they wanted the islands of Japan.

The Mongols were fierce warriors, but they were not water people. Despite the thunderclouds, they set sail across the gray waters in thousands of boats to conquer the islands.

The people of Japan said Raijin, the god of lighting, thunder, and storms, sent the divine wind Kamikaze to save them. The great winds blew and tore apart the Mongol fleet, flinging boats and men and their banner flags like grains of sand in the sea.

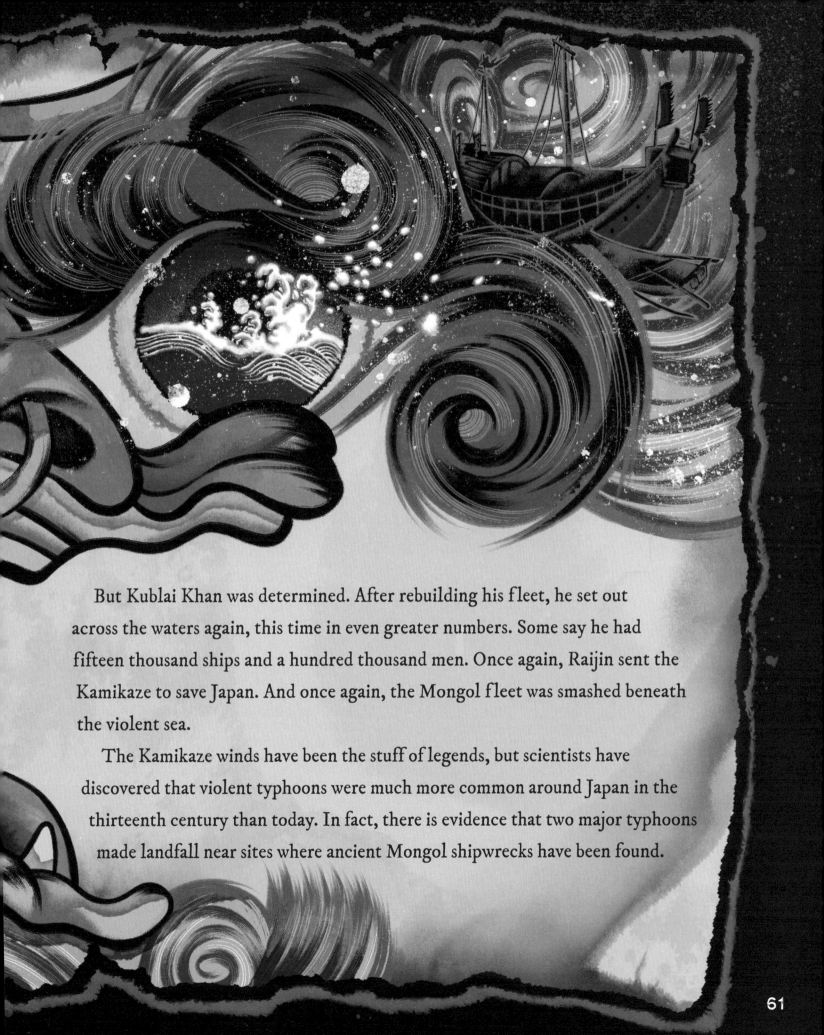

But Kublai Khan was determined. After rebuilding his fleet, he set out across the waters again, this time in even greater numbers. Some say he had fifteen thousand ships and a hundred thousand men. Once again, Raijin sent the Kamikaze to save Japan. And once again, the Mongol fleet was smashed beneath the violent sea.

The Kamikaze winds have been the stuff of legends, but scientists have discovered that violent typhoons were much more common around Japan in the thirteenth century than today. In fact, there is evidence that two major typhoons made landfall near sites where ancient Mongol shipwrecks have been found.

# SAND-BUILDING

Of all the things I love on this planet, sand may be my favorite. I can build mighty waves at sea, but they last only briefly. However, sand and I have been building and shaping the world for millions of years. Sand and I, we understand each other.

Together, we shape towering crescents, taller than your buildings. Or maybe we'll sculpt long, low ridges that shift like serpents across the land as far as the eye can see. In some places, we can even make the dunes sing.

Together, we rush over rocks and hillsides, endlessly, endlessly brushing away the softer stone. Sculpting and smoothing until all that remains are strange and magical shapes.

**DUNES** are large masses of windblown sand. Every dune has a windward side and a slip face. Sand is blown or pushed up the windward side and slides down the slip face, which is usually steeper and smoother.

The Badain Jaran Desert, China, is known for its SINGING SANDS. Its dunes make a strange moaning in the wind and are some of the tallest in the world, reaching 1,600 feet (490 meters).

**WIND EROSION** is caused by sand and other rough particles carried by the wind. Like sandpaper, the gritty wind gradually wears away softer rock, leaving only the harder rock standing. This process is also called Aeolian erosion, named after Aeolus, the ancient Greek Keeper of the Winds.

**FAIRY CHIMNEYS**
of Cappadocia, Turkey

HOODOOS in Bisti/
De-Na-Zin Wilderness Area
in New Mexico, USA.

MUSHROOM ROCKS in
White Desert National Park, Egypt

# SANDSTORMS

The people of the seas and the deserts have always loved me best. Or perhaps they have feared me the most. I've told you what I can do at sea. Now let me show you my power with sand.

First, my Simoom, my "poison wind." I come rushing hot and dry, like a living furnace with burning clouds of dust. Kings have declared war on my Simoom and marched their armies against me. They were never seen again.

Next, my Haboob. This one comes after a thunderstorm. When the thunderclouds collapse, I burst from the bottom, scoop every grain of sand and dust, and then rise up again into a wall of hard-blowing grit.

My Brickfielder comes after a drought, when the earth has been burnt to red dust. The red winds swallow cities.

And of course, my Khamsin, which rages with burning sand for fifty days, give or take.

**SANDSTORMS AND DUST STORMS**
occur in dry, hot areas where the ground is
covered with sand or dusty soil, rather than rock
or vegetation. In deserts or dusty areas that are
suffering a drought, the sand and dust are easy for
the wind to pick up and can hang in the sky like a
blanket. Sandstorms can be extremely dangerous,
filled with blinding, choking dust and sand.

The biggest migration in the world isn't done by wildebeests or butterflies; it's done by dust.

Every year, winds pick up millions of tons of dust and sand from the Saharan desert and blow it across the Atlantic Ocean to the Americas. Scientists estimate 182 million tons of the Saharan desert migrate every year — that's enough to fill 689,290 semitrucks.

The dust is carried high up into the atmosphere and catches the trade winds westward, across the Atlantic Ocean, curving over the Amazon Rainforest and up across the Caribbean Sea. As the giant plume of dust travels with the winds, it sprinkles down, bringing life-giving minerals to faraway animals and plants.

As the dust falls over the Atlantic, it feeds ocean creatures with essential minerals such as iron and phosphorus. The mineral-rich dust may cause algae

blooms that lower oxygen levels in the waters. It may also soak up moist air over the Atlantic and help tear apart baby hurricanes before they get too big.

Phosphorus is especially important for plant growth. But in the Amazon Rainforest, it quickly drains from the soil with heavy rains and flooding. Without the Saharan dust, the rainforest would starve, especially the air plants living high up in the canopy.

The dusty winds continue to curve northward to fertilize the waters and coral reefs of the Caribbean Sea. Finally, they carry over Puerto Rico and the southern United States, sprinkling red Saharan dust over cities, clogging the air with pollutants, and creating beautiful streaky red sunsets.

# You Know Me

Without me there would be no deserts.
No waves. No sailing ships.

Without me the world would be hushed and still. No
smells would carry. No seeds would scatter. No fogs or
smokes would be blown clear.

When I whistle, the world breathes afresh. I bring the
possibility of something new, of hope and disaster.

And when I rush over the hills and through the trees
and you feel my power, you know me. Because you are a
part of me, and I am part of you.

# INDEX OF KEY TERMS

# FURTHER READING

Bone, Emily. *Look Inside: Wild Weather*. Illustrated by Bao Luu. London: Usborne Books, 2020

Gooley, Tristan. *The Secret World of Weather: How to Read Sign in Every Cloud, Breeze, Hill, Street, Plant, Animal, and Dewdrop*. New York: The Experiment, 2021.

DK. *Hurricane and Tornado*. London, DK Children, 2021

Reed, MK. *Science Comics: Wild Weather: Storms, Meteorology, and Climate* Illustrated by Jonathan Hill. New York: First Second Books, 2019

RACHEL POLIQUIN is an award-winning author of more than ten nonfiction books about science and nature for kids, including *The Museum of Odd Body Leftovers*, *How to Promenade with a Python (and not get eaten)*, and *The Strangest Thing in the Sea*. She lives in Vancouver, British Columbia, with her husband and three children.

RACHEL WADA was born in Japan, grew up briefly in Hong Kong and China, and now lives and works in Vancouver, British Columbia. She started drawing at a very young age, perhaps as a way of transcending the language barriers of the cities she grew up in. Rachel's cultural roots and upbringing continue to inspire her work to this day. She graduated with a B.F.A. in illustration from Emily Carr University of Art + Design in 2016. Her children's book debut, *The Phonebooth in Mr. Hirota's Garden* written by Heather Smith, was shortlisted for the Pacific Northwest Book Award. Rachel's work can also be found in newspapers, magazines, and online publications.